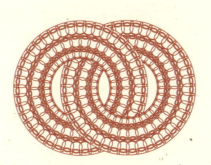

THE LAST BEAST WE REVEL IN

THE
LAST BEAST
WE REVEL IN

NOAH DAVIS

CavanKerry
PRESS

Copyright © 2025 by Noah Davis

All rights reserved. No part of this book may be used, reproduced, or adapted to public performances in any manner whatsoever without permission from the publisher, except in the case of brief quotations embodied in critical articles and reviews. For more information, write to Permissions, CavanKerry Press, 5 Horizon Road #2403, Fort Lee, New Jersey 07024.

CavanKerry Press Ltd.
Fort Lee, New Jersey
www.cavankerrypress.org

Publisher's Cataloging-in-Publication Data
provided by Five Rainbows Cataloging Services
Names: Davis, Noah, 1995- author.
Title: The last beast we revel in / Noah Davis.
Description: Fort Lee, NJ : CavanKerry Press, 2025.
Identifiers: ISBN 978-1-960327-10-9 (paperback)
Subjects: LCSH: Appalachian Region--Poetry. | Ecology--Poetry
    Natural history--Poetry. |Family life--Poetry. American poetry. |
    BISAC: POETRY / American / General. | POETRY /
    Subjects & Themes / Animals & Nature. | POETRY /
    Subjects & Themes / Family. | SPORTS & RECREATION / Hunting.
Classification: LCC PS283.O3 L37 2025 (print) | LCC PS283.O3 (ebook) |
    DDC 811/.6--dc23.

Cover artwork: "Dog on a Log" by Winslow Homer
Cover design by Coral Sue Black
Interior text design by Natasha Kane
First Edition 2025, Printed in the United States of America

CavanKerry Press is dedicated to springboarding the careers of previously unpublished, early, and midcareer poets with our Emerging Voices series.

 Made possible by funds from the New Jersey State Council on the Arts, a partner agency of the National Endowment for the Arts.

CavanKerry Press is grateful for the generous support it receives from the New Jersey State Council on the Arts, as well as the following funders:

The Academy of American Poets
Community of Literary Magazines and Presses
National Book Foundation
New Jersey Arts and Culture Renewal Fund
New Jersey Economic Development Authority
The Poetry Foundation

Also by Noah Davis

Of This River (2020)
A Literary Field Guide to Northern Appalachia,
　　coedited with Todd Davis and Carolyn Mahan (2024)

For my Beloved, Family, and Home

From whose flanks comes this world's dark lowing?
  —Gabrielle Calvocoressi

Contents

After felling every beetle-blighted ash on the ridge	3
How Blood Becomes the River	4
Places Familiar	5
The September Side of Light	6
Poem Found on Three Springs Run	9
I Ask What We Are	10
Heron Heart	12
Appalachian Lust Song	13
Mountain Salve	14
Conception	15
Trout Heart	16
Portrait of the Beloved with Rain	17
What I Hear as Crow Song	18
Genesis	19
On the last day of rifle season	20
Penance	21
Telling My Beloved What I Lost on the Mountain	22
Arguing Again in the Afternoon	23
Hound Heart	24
Poem Sewn into My Hunting Jacket	25
In April with my beloved	26

≈

Prayer for the People Who Pulled the Mountaintops Back Like a Fingernail	29
With My Beloved Upon Waking from a Nap in a Field a Week Before the First Haying	30
July Drought	31
Tick Triptych	32
The morning after my mother saw my beloved and me sleeping in the same bed	35
Mercy Song	36

March	37
My Brother and I Watch Dogs Chase Trains over the Pig Hole Bridge	38
In Bed with My Beloved and an Elk Leg	39
Human Heart	40
I like to believe	41
Wedding Poem	42
Poem Sewn into My Briar Pants	43
Solstice Bluegills	44
Here, Long Before My Father's Death	45
Pink Lady Slipper	46
Mother	47
Bee Heart	48
My Beloved Asks	49
Marriage Poem	50
From the valley	51
God came to me on County Road 26	52
Think of Lips and What Earth Needs for Vegetables	53
My brother fought	54
Dream with My Beloved and Honeycomb Ending with a Line from Yeats	55
My father gives me a knife	56

❧

The Last Beast We Revel In	59
Acknowledgments	71

After felling every beetle-blighted ash on the ridge

we lie down while moth wings beat
the window like children's hands
and I cup the egg of your ankle
bone in my mouth, now safe
from shattering.

How Blood Becomes the River

Metal settles at the lowest point

                              —the bottom of tunnels or in the belly

meat of bluegills—

                flowing with rain

                          and thaw. Rivers of iron fill the spaces

between the rocks we've broken.

Places Familiar

Meth labs explode in towns of people I love.
Great aunts and uncles, in-laws and second cousins.

They walk in the night to the fire. Down the alley
or around the block. Gathered with neighbors

in flickering light. Wondering how many were inside.
If they'd recognize them from the gas station.

Knew them from behind the counter
at the cafeteria, passing Jell-O or tapioca.

After the fire, teeth are all that are
familiar. Because everyone here smiles

with their mouths closed, the people I love
walk home counting in their heads

what neighbors they couldn't find
in the dark.

The September Side of Light

On the day no deer dies in the county

      and every bear finds enough acorns to eat

then sleeps the rest of the afternoon into night

      where they see stars shaped in their image,

my beloved and I pick the last tomatoes

      hanging like slow dripping water

and bring the bread from the kitchen

      and lie in the yard watching two crows

who we have named and who have named us

      fly from the neighbor's yard where they talked with him

while he dug the carrots his husband planted before he died in May,

      and the neighbor didn't wash the dirt from the sweet orange skin before he chewed,

smiling up at the birds with brown and orange flecks between his teeth,

      and now the two crows land on the house of the thirty-seven-year-old woman

who hasn't remembered her uncle's hand on her thirteen-year-old-self in almost four days as she makes a bowl of kettle

corn popped in coconut oil and sugar and thinks she'll walk to the
bridge

    and count the shadows of fish drifting across the sandy
        bottom,

and maybe, if it's not too late when she arrives home,

    she'll call the man who gave her his number at the
        supermarket

next to the little tubs of caramel for dipping apples,

    and my beloved and I hang between their yards,

having already forgiven each other for the words said in the tenor

    of talus slopes this morning over oatmeal, and we eat the
        heavy bread

and chew for so long that we must start a new conversation

    every time we swallow, such good, dense bread that jaws
        ache

in eating, and we welcome the ease of sun-warmed tomatoes,

    and tell each other tomato stories, tilling and planting and
        picking

and eating, more tomato stories than we knew we carried,

    and in this discovery revel until we each, separately,

and in two different moments, realize the warmth and release of tomatoes between our teeth is the same as our feasting

on the softest, most tender parts of our bodies, and being pulled by that want,

climb to the room with the windows facing joyfully west,

and lie together in that light different from the day before,

and detached from tomorrow's light, when deer will die,

and bears will wander hungry, and crows will not come to their names,

but that time is far from our laying, and this room,

and the hundred more stories, heavy like tomatoes,

swaying on the September side of light.

Poem Found on Three Springs Run

Before the creek goes underground,
I'm hung between the sun clinging
to the riffle above me
and the moon below,
between the light that sticks
to fingers and the back
of my beloved's neck
where skin meets shoulder
and I, like water through
this hollow, follow
the crease to the unbraided
language she speaks.

I Ask What We Are

What part of morning?

                                                   What bread?

            What strip-mining site?

                                  What stream turned to acid?

                   What caddis?

What fish swimming sideways?

                                  What hawk?

            What updraft?

                        What fire?

                                      What rock?

What moth?

                  What finger?

What blade?

What berry?

What bone?

Heron Heart

I'm thankful my beloved's heart
was more patient than any mink
on the river, and even though
I swam out and into her riffle
like a nervous trout, she waited
for me to find my lie then held
me there with a stare I prayed
would linger like a thin bone
caught at the back of my throat.

Appalachian Lust Song

I want my mouth
full of wet river stone.

Mountain Salve

My beloved crushes nettles
into red sauce when her muscles
ache, chews fennel
when her stomach roils,
and when I slice my thumb
like the ripest plum
she wraps its two halves
in burdock leaves until the wound
fills quick as silt sluffing off
the clear-cut hills
our great-grandfathers left us
to live beneath.

Conception

Tonight, you bury me
in you like a hellbender

            creased in rocks
            under the bank

until you're finished
burying

            and I've spilled
            all I can and fall

out like a hellbender
from between rocks.

            We lie on the floor and I speak
            of the salamander and his slime

and those living rocks
and you tell me your dog

            swallowed a salamander
            when you were eight,

that all you will think
of until morning

            is froth at the mouth
            and the whites of dogs' eyes.

Trout Heart

I've been told the heart
will run out of blood but I doubt it.
          —Jim Harrison

When the trout is hooked deep
in his throat and held above the river,

water on his jaw is first more water
than blood, then more blood

than water, until only water is left.
But if the heart does run out of blood,

will the muscle accept water?
I love myself enough to believe

my heart is a trout. The trout in my beloved's
chest is of the same small stream as mine.

Can you tell me how many years
it will take for trout and all other

gilled things to swim without blood?
I think, one day, enough of us will

have died in rivers that hearts can soak
under stones and young people will hand

each other warm, waterlogged hearts,
which become the trout in their chests:

the bleeding fish with tails
kicking out into the current,

fading white bellies rising
toward the cradled moon.

Portrait of the Beloved with Rain

Today, I saw ice in the shape of her shoulder blades hanging from a log above a riffle in the stream. Tonight, as my tongue finds that cold again, I shiver at the body betraying its name. Her legs: corded like running sap from a gash on a maple's bark. Stomach: the glide in a river clean enough that I eat the fish and lie in the current until the sky is so full of stars I can't find my way to shore. My beloved does with me what rain does with streams.

What I Hear as Crow Song

Wet pavement rides the ridges up

        to where the forest breaks like hair

when the taut newness of a scar

        writes that desire is black feathers

caught in the heads of dried goldenrod,

        that hunger's blue lines run over hands

and between knuckles, that death, after rain,

        leaks its sweet smell through the river

of your teeth.

Genesis

A black bear stands
              on two legs.

The image in which
              we were made.

On the last day of rifle season

deer come off the ridge,
                    like sisters

          who haven't stood
          in the same room
          in fifteen years,

              distrusting

                          every step and sound.

Penance

Last night, the word *nipple* found
my mouth the same way humming
birds find cardinal flowers, and I was taken
by my beloved to where mules walk
the shore of a lake that breathes
green glass from churches at the bottom of
what fifty years ago was
a valley.

I spoke to a mule in the timbre
of truck tires on cattle guards
and asked him to take back my words,
slick as river stone and rippled,
and keep them on the shore
far away from my drowning mouth.

Telling My Beloved What I Lost on the Mountain

I lifted the two fawns
out of the dead doe's body
and left them in
the purple sleeve
where she made them
and poured the milk
she leaked from her nipples
onto my palm
and over their shivering.

Arguing Again in the Afternoon

Like nettles in drought
and blue jay feathers in rain
neither of us gave
to the other.

Hound Heart

Beloved, the hound
in my chest scrambles
into the absence of you.

A redbone tumbling
after a bear is the only
chase close to the careening
I do through the ravine
of memory your hands
carved in me.

You ought to be here
to quell this dog
and his raking.
He's scraped away
all the tracks in the clay
of my chest.

Save me from his flailing.

Poem Sewn into My Hunting Jacket

When I say I am going to kill a deer on the mountain,
    I mean I want our daughter to have the strength to
        jump fences,
and when she doesn't come home at night, we will know to
   find her
       in the neighbor's garden.

When I say we will know to find her in the neighbor's
    garden,
       I mean we will not worry about her in strangers'
          houses.
Because while she grew in you, I carried a deer down
       from the mountain, then fed you that deer so she could
be woven with the folding knowledge of the woods,
      which is always unfolding.

When I say we will find her in the neighbor's garden,
      I mean she has the strength to jump fences,
and when I am weak with age, she will walk into the folding
      woods and kill a deer on the mountain.

In April with my beloved

I find the skeletons of deer that died
by the stream and sit watching purple moths
crawl down the long slides of their spines.

This is the endless heaven I've dreamed of.
You and I. Our spines. Purple moths following
the emptied hollows of our bones. Wings thin as milk.

三

Prayer for the People Who Pulled the Mountaintops Back Like a Fingernail

When you die,
may bees build
honeycomb
in your skulls.

With My Beloved Upon Waking from a Nap in a Field a Week Before the First Haying

Mulberry-purple-bird-shit-love.

    Trout-cut-open-to-pink-love.

Fresh-split-locust-posts-tan-in-the-afternoon-love.

    White-goats-milk-on-your-oats-love.

Deer-swimming-through-deep-water-love.

    Black-crow-never-forgets-your-face-love.

Don't-leave-me-in-this-tall-grass-love.

July Drought

Heat lightning

                brightens

     the black

                    between

clouds.

A deep

                    rushing.

    An even deeper

absence.

Tick Triptych

I.

I've checked my father's body
for ticks every day this May,
and again, tonight, I press
my forefinger against the mole
on his left hamstring
below the buttock,
and again, it is not ridged,
nor legged, and again, I find
my father's body unfamiliar,
the same way my body must be to him,
grown far from the part of himself
he left in my mother.

II.

Out of fear, and our own want to feast,
my beloved and I strip in the bathroom.
I search her ginseng-flower flesh
and she inspects my trout-backed
skin for parasites that would take the blood
we'd promised each other that morning,
as we had every morning since
the mild winters began
and we realized how difficult
this promise would be to keep
with the woods wrecked full
of waiting mouths.

III.

The swollen tick dangles
like a fat earring
from my lobe.
In drinking,
the tick is now
more me
than it,
but still
I crush the part
that is not me.

**The morning after my mother saw my beloved and me
   sleeping in the same bed**

I ate grapes that sagged
in their skins. Sweet turned
like horses against sleet.

Mercy Song

Money enough for nail polish

and time enough to paint my beloved's fingers

and light enough to find her blackberry-black mouth

and sense enough to not drive home

and awake enough to walk on the other side of the guardrail

and sober enough to name it *moon*

and sad enough to cry over car-struck catbirds

and tired enough to sleep here

                                      until all this mercy

runs out.

March

I listened in the dark
as the river ice
buckled like a hundred
trees snapping.

The great sheets thick as my chest
razored the banks, a power
as strange and disarming
as an ancient army.

And I imagined bears asleep
on the mountain waking
to the sound, the splintering
entry of another year, then
closing their eyes again.

My Brother and I Watch Dogs Chase Trains over the Pig Hole Bridge

Dogs chase trains, never realizing trains have no lungs.

With the summer fires, we breathe air the color of dogs.

We pray like the dogs who chase trains.

Faithful that when this lungless thing does not stop,
    another will come.

In Bed with My Beloved and an Elk Leg

When I reach for you,
hours away from both ends
of light, you say your first thought
is the elk leg dropped at our truck
last month by a dog
we'd never met.

You ask what other animals
have brought me the parts
of other animals.
I say the elk leg was for both
of us and move my palm
over your knee.

You say that my leg was the first
you were ever freely given.
No other animal need carry
me in their mouth
to you.

Human Heart

The people who kept the people poor
and made them shave the mountain
found no hearts like theirs, and now,
when it rains, the orange left by coal
flows down the mountain like my beloved's hair.

In this hollow the color of my beloved's hair,
we found our hearts, familiar and red,
like the broad-winged hawk's cry, high
and two-noted.

I like to believe

my mother pulled my brother
and me from herself

the same way her cousins
lifted snapping turtles, quick

and tail first, from the oil drums
that lined the east side

of the wooden garage
where the hoop was nailed

too high above the gravel to reach,
so she shot the basketball

into the water-filled barrels,
each time daring the turtles

to bite the ball, each time daring
herself to lose a finger.

Wedding Poem

Turtle eaten

from turtle shell:
                       summer bowl carved by spring mouths.

We will clean this bone together.

Fill it when we are hungry.

Poem Sewn into My Briar Pants

When I say I am going to pick raspberries by the train
    tracks,
        I mean I want our son's fingers to be stained purple.

When I say I want our son's fingers to be stained purple,
        I mean I want him to know how pinched berries
            bleed on his thumb.

When I say I want him to know how pinched berries bleed
    on his thumb,
        I mean I want him to see the blood he pulled from
            you.

When I say I want him to see the blood he pulled from you,
        I mean I want him to see the blood of mothers in
            others,

to touch them in the same way we've taught
        him to pick raspberries.

Solstice Bluegills

After my brother and I drowned
the last worm we packed to the pond,
we found wild strawberries
blinking like brake lights on the bank.
He tried first, catching fish with fruit,
and because the bluegills were as mortal as us
they couldn't refuse the color, the sweet,
a berry offered only in June
when light is longest.

Here, Long Before My Father's Death

I've started to walk downstream of my father,

so when his dying comes, I'll be knocked

from my step, and he'll show me the current

that has carried most of this mountain away.

Pink Lady Slipper

Quiet lungs fill with air.

        Red veins empty of blood.

Mother

My mother killed the last lion
on our mountain

and fed my father, brother,
and me the body bit by bit.

My mother is a woman who loved
horses enough to kill lions.

No matter how few lions.
No matter how many horses.

Bee Heart

We bend like a serviceberry branch
heavy with a honey swarm. A thousand
humming hearts on a single branch.
How can we refuse such bending?

My Beloved Asks

Why wake in the night?

      Why lie in the grass?

           Why hoe in the dark?

                 Why wear clothes?

                      Why bring a carrot

covered in dirt?

Marriage Poem

The legs of late
November light
casting shadows
on the broken floor
remind me
of when we
were deer.

From the valley

we watch a storm collapse
on the mountain
like those ancient pigeons
who once flew in rivers
over the earth
dropping to roost,
reveling in the grief
that even clouds, like birds,
are shredded by these ridges.

God came to me on County Road 26

and lifted her doe head to offer
me her fur throat.

Blood pumped in lung-rhythm,
from her nose, fountained
by my truck's bumper.

I cut God's throat,
and her warmth melted the snow.

I eat God each day and pray
in the way she taught me:
catching her breath in my lungs.

Think of Lips and What Earth Needs for Vegetables

I'm probably not the only man
who while turning compost
was told by the ant-stripped cantaloupe
rinds and browned bell peppers
to press my lips to the soft
between my beloved's legs
and say the word *fecundity*.

Fe-cun-di-ty.

Like broccoli going to flower.
Like boxelder beetles on garlic chives.
Like mourning doves flushed
from beneath the weighted
head of a sunflower
in late September.

My brother fought

with the rage of railroad tracks
and cheekbones. On Tuesday

night his left canine was
a drop of milk in his palm.

Dream with My Beloved and Honeycomb Ending with a Line from Yeats

We lay in the grass for a month
and bees built honeycomb

around our bodies. She told me
we shouldn't peel the wax

from our shoulders
because we'd pull ourselves

from this place where
we found each other

entangled in the field
neither of us knew before,

but now lie, coffined and warm,
in the bee-loud glade.

My father gives me a knife

and says

      if I fall

it will go

      through

my heart.

The Last Beast We Revel In

In the dark, before the sun has spilled its yolk
over the lip of the ridge to remind us how young

all the trees are in this reef of the world,
we follow taillights up Laurel Mountain

the same way we follow wives and girlfriends
down hallways or upstairs to bed, always within

an arm's length, but with enough space to brake
before crashing. It's so dark the world could be whole

again. With no town at the low point in this valley,
and only the sound of dogs restless in their cages,

like water boiling in a kettle—we can lay
the belief, dumb on our tongues,

that this is where we began
our walking upright on earth.

We've brought our wives and girlfriends,
and in the blue light of the dashboard,

steam from coffee catches in their eyelashes
the way oil slicks catch in an eddy.

We talk about bears and dogs.
How we need dogs to kill bears.

How dogs want to kill bears.
We talk to these women

we've buried ourselves in.
Swallowed cups of them.

Said sentences like,
I need you in my mouth

like milk. And we've
been laughed at and slapped

and kissed because of those sentences.
But now we're waiting for the night

to break, for that dog with the best nose
in someone else's truck to smell where the bear

stepped. We wait for this dog to cross the trail
of the bear and howl a sound like a deer's heart tearing

around a bullet. A howl that sends all our hearts
along the line of trucks scrambling toward the bawl.

We bring our wives and girlfriends
and they bring our children who doze

in the backseat like doves on a wire, heads dipping
and swaying against the strength of their necks.

Our children love us and our dogs.
We want our children to love killing bears.

Now the sun has soaked the top of the ridge,
and through the open windows we see how thin

all the trees are, just the tops of the branches:
veins in the sky's eye. Because the hound bays

like its heart was torn last night, just when the dark
was darker, the man with the best-nosed hound

unlatches the cage of his other hounds,
and they spin out and away into witch hazel

and rhododendron. The orange forest of November,
stiff with frost-heaves, breaks like tiny bells

beneath the dogs' weight. We hear their howling
disappear and we long for their calling,

which we've held close since we woke in the valley
and climbed to where the bears live, high above us.

The radio in the dogs' collars sends the purple trail
of their track back to the screens we hold in our hands.

The purple lines, like the streaming tendrils
on the tongue petals of white violets, paint

the ache hooked in the dog's noses, wrenching
them forward toward the bear, whose dread

the hounds smell, and we watch
on the screens in our palms

as the bear careens through groves
of fox grapes along south-facing slopes.

Our grandfathers and our great-grandfathers
left us mountains shorter than they were given.

They stood in front of the downed chestnuts
and sawn hemlocks for pictures, like they were posing

on Easter in front of a church. They carried coal
into the day and said the dark beneath the earth

had a weight of its own, that hell's probably not full of flames,
but a place where all the light in the world recedes

behind you. They brought the dark back with them
and washed in the yard with the hose until the grass died,

choked on coal dust. We learned from the sprinkled
shapes on their sheets that our fathers still carried

bits of grit when they slept with our mothers.
They passed that coal to us in our mother's

bellies, and we were born with flecked blood.
Grains grinding between molars, dust

sifting behind eyes, sleep tinted
with the half-remembered colors

of blue jays our fathers carried
with them into the mine.

There's nothing left for us to sell:
mountain hollow like a snail's shell.

We fear our feet might break
through the crust. Every company

left an iron-rusted stream
behind it. The reservoir glows

in the night. We work above ground now.
Sitting and standing until our feet flatten

and our asses ache. We drive truck
for the plate glass factory, work the line

at the fracking repair plant. Some of us ride
the railroad, a few teach. One man learned

to cut meat and offers chicken, turkey,
pig, cow, deer, bear across a steel counter.

Our wives and girlfriends work as secretaries
or look after children at the day care,

some stand stirring vats at the sauce factory
until tomato and oregano stain their skin.

There's a new dust in all of us
sent by the lights we work under.

The first pack is spent,
bear far ahead of the dogs.

We pitch new dogs on the trail,
mouths wet as tomatoes in August.

We snatch the waning dogs by the collars.
Voices hoarse, ears and tails bleeding

from multiflora rose. Dogs drink and eat in cages
lined with soft straw. Their ribs jut, like train

tracks out from the plain of their sides.
We blot and tape their bleeding while we wait

for the fresh dogs to atlas the path of the bear.
The hounds sprint away, and purple lines grow

like wrinkles in the sun. A smaller bear
would've treed, scampered up a tulip poplar,

shimmied up a birch to a *Y* of branches,
believing the dogs would leave.

We've shot bears from trees,
like the biggest birds in the world.

While the bears wait to be shot, mouths
slack open, slobber drips like icicles in the sun.

We've seen the bullet entering and exiting
the bear's chest without binoculars.

Bear faltering on a limb, clawing against
his own falling, at his own disbelief at our reach.

We witness ourselves in the bear that falls.
Arms stretching, legs pedaling.

We don't confess we see a human
shape in the bear's shape.

The bear's already above the road.
We hear the dogs on the spine

of the ridge, us on the bench, the mountain's
insides mined like the memory of our grandmothers.

This bear gallops. A bear that if the evening
light was pink, we'd believe he was a horse.

None of us would shoot a horse. Our grandfathers
told the story of the circus train that crashed

in the year they reached the age they stopped wishing
for the circus train, and of all the horses and zebras

and camels they shot with their fathers as the animals crawled
broken-bodied from the splintered boxcars

toward the mountain. The ringmaster,
in his Brooklyn Dodgers cap, told our grandfathers

and great-grandfathers to eat what they could cut away.
We see on our screens that the bear crosses Horse Tooth Run.

The hounds run up the stream to the next ridge.
We drive off Laurel Mountain, and back up Buck Mountain,

radio antennas bent like the skeletons of goldenrod
after an ice storm, hoping to beat the bear

to the top. Pistols at our sides and rifles, silent and clean,
propped between legs. We keep parts of the bears

we kill. Claws hang from a rope off the bedframe, bleached-
white skulls on the shelves, like books we've never read.

We've watched bears tumble, so exhausted the dogs
are on their heels, on top of their heels, riding their heels,

and the shooter must lead the shot so the bear
intercepts the bullet, somersaulting over himself.

We throw more dogs in the chase.
The final three fresh dogs on the mountain,

who've whined since the first howl this morning,
who've bruised their noses on the bars of their cages.

Our wives and girlfriends clip the leashes
around their shoulders, across their chests

like the sashes they wore
on homecoming night.

We were awkward in our loving on the nights
we pulled the sashes off their shoulders.

Unfamiliar with clothes that left glitter
on our hands like ice on wet skin.

Children in the backseat play with the button
of their knife sheaths we gave them for birthdays.

They unfold the blades and whittle their fingernails,
learn what parts of themselves don't feel pain.

Our killing this bear is an old thing.
We have no more trees

that could be churches.
No mammoths left.

No elk on this plateau.
All the bison stampeded

off cliffs and shot from trains.
Wolves poisoned.

Mountain lions run down by hounds.
The bear is the last beast we revel in.

The dogs mill above us. Purple lines on our screens
puddle as they weave around each other. Then each dog

disappears into the white and we panic. We grab rifles
and run to the last place we trusted our dogs.

In the mine's gullet, we hear our dogs, like a couple
three doors down. We breathe on the wrecked chin

of the mine the company forgot to close.
Bear hair on dog hair in the prints.

We wait on the broken cheek of the mine,
knowing we won't follow the bear or our dogs,

fearing we'll fall down a shaft and die.
We take turns calling the names of the dogs

that our children have come to love,
our children weeping. Our screens are white

like a bloodroot blossom. The first hound climbs up out
of the tunnel. Its green eyes bob in our flashlights

beneath the black coal dust caking its feet, legs,
cheeks. Tongue caged in its mouth, eyes shuttering

from the light. We leash the dog to the oldest
tree on the ridge, fifty years round,

all its leaves dropped. The pan of water
we set in front of the dog plumes

with coal dust from its tongue. After ten minutes,
another hound moans out the throat of the mine.

Our children wipe their eyes and refill the pans
when the water's too black to see the silver

bottom. Hound after hound tails out
of the tunnel's mouth and our children ruin

six towels cleaning the faces of the dogs.
We hear the final hound in the dark.

A Plott. Which means the bear is still alive
because a Plott will not leave a bear

unless the bear is dead. We hear the Plott and rush
to our guns. Our wives and girlfriends push the children

back and grab their guns. The dogs that were silent
in the slack of fatigue whine and yelp. Our fingers bend

on triggers, though we see no bear. The Plott is so close
we can hear it snarl on the bear's arm, a skip in the record

of its bark. The bear backs the hound out of the mine.
He knows we're waiting for him to climb out

into the light. We're waiting for the sound
to become flesh in the shape of the bear our hearts

have painted. We each pray we'll be the one to kill
the bear. The Plott's tail flicks out of the mine's mouth

like a snake's tongue. We almost shoot the hound,
but the hound rushes aside as the bear surfaces

from the hole. The bear's so silent we question
if he left that part of himself in the mine.

We wait for the bear to tumble toward the trees beyond us.
Three steps out of the mine we shoot the bear.

Three quick shots to stop his step.
He falls hard on the leaf duff,

and before he dies, we shoot him again
just behind the skull to stop the jaws that chew the air.

We huddle around the bear covered
in the coal dust that rubs onto our hands

as we cradle the head and pose for pictures
like our great-grandfathers posed in front

of chestnut trunks, and we imagine driving
home to our fathers to show them what else

we pulled from the mountain
the company said was empty.

Acknowledgments

My thanks to the editors of the following journals and publications in which these poems first appeared, sometimes in different forms:

About Place: "Prayer for the People Who Pulled the Mountain Tops Back Like a Fingernail"
Appalachia: "Heron Heart"
Birmingham Poetry Review: "Places Familiar," "Solstice Bluegills"
Chautauqua: "The September Side of Light," "Tick Triptych"
Cumberland River Review: "Penance"
The Fourth River: "Arguing Again in the Afternoon," "Mountain Salve"
The Hiram Poetry Review: "Mercy Song"
The Hollins Critic: "Bee Heart"
Kestrel: "Here, Long Before My Father's Death"
Nimrod: "Trout Heart"
Northern Appalachia Review: "Portrait of the Beloved with Rain"
North American Review: "Marriage Poem"
Pine Mountain Sand & Gravel: "God came to me on County Road 26" (as "God Came to Me")
Poetry East: "Dream with my Beloved and Honeycomb Ending with a Line from Yeats"
Spillway: "Mother"
Sport Literate: "I like to believe"
Southern Humanities Review: "The Last Beast We Revel In"
Talking River Review: "In April with my beloved," "Poem Sewn into my Briar Pants"
Terrain.org: "After felling every beetle-blighted ash on the ridge," "Poem Found on Three Springs Run," "Poem Sewn into My Hunting Jacket"

THRUSH: "Appalachian Lust Song," "The Morning After My Mother Saw the Beloved and I Sleeping in the Same Bed"

"Bee Heart," "Dream with My Beloved and Honeycomb Ending with a Line from Yeats," and "From the valley" were reprinted in the limited edition quire "Even While the Moon Is Young" (Bear Scratch Press, 2024).

"Poem Sewn into My Hunting Jacket" was reprinted in *Attached to the Living World: A New Ecopoetry Anthology*, edited by Ann Fisher-Wirth and Laura-Gray Street (Trinity University Press, 2025).

"Solstice Bluegills" was reprinted by Anglers Journal.

"The Last Beast We Revel In" was a finalist for the 2021 Auburn Witness Poetry Prize.

Thank you to the public lands and waters of Pennsylvania.

Thank you to Indiana University, and my time in Bloomington, where many of these poems were written in the apartment on North College Avenue.

Thank you to the following folks for their love as I make poems: David and Jodi, Tanya and Wendell, Dave, Bruce, and Marcia, David, Taylor, Christine, Michael, Bob, Chris, DJD, Kurt and Carolyn, Henry, Michael, Doug and Sue, Alex, Sean, Joe, Aimee, Jack, Scott and Ruth, Derek, and David and Gary. Thank you, Meredith, Soleil, Alberto, Austin, janan, and L. for your love and attentiveness toward these poems. So happy our poem-lives are entwined.

Thank you, Adrian, Ross, and Cathy, for asking questions as my thesis became this manuscript. I hope you see your own breath in these poems.

Thank you to CavanKerry Press. A dream. A true dream.

Thank you to my editor, Gabriel Cleveland, for your kindness, close reading, and championing of these poems. I will forever remember the phone call.

Thank you, Nathan, for being my brother. We have many waters to fish.

Thank you, Mom, for being my mother. We have many hours to talk.

Thank you, Dad, for being my father. We have many poems to read to each other.

Thank you, jewelweed, Nikea. We have many gardens ahead.

Thank you to the mountains, rivers, animals, birds, and fish.

Never-ending thankfulness.

CavanKerry's Mission

A not-for-profit literary press serving art and community, CavanKerry is committed to expanding the reach of poetry and other fine literature to a general readership by publishing works that explore the emotional and psychological landscapes of everyday life, and to bringing that art to the underserved where they live, work, and receive services.

Other Books in the Emerging Voices Series

Beyond the Watershed, Nadia Alexis
In Inheritance of Drowning, Dorsía Smith Silva
Seraphim, Angelique Zobitz
When Did We Stop Being Cute?, Martin Wiley
Boy, Tracy Youngblom
In the River of Songs, Susan Jackson
Mausoleum of Flowers, Daniel B. Summerhill
A Half-Life, David S. Cho
Uncertain Acrobats, Rebecca Hart Olander
Her Kind, Cindy Veach
Deke Dangle Dive, Gibson Fay-LeBlanc
Pelted by Flowers, Kali Lightfoot
Rise Wildly, Tina Kelley
Set in Stone, Kevin Carey
Scraping Away, Fred Shaw
Rewilding, January Gill O'Neil
My Oceanography, Harriet Levin
See the Wolf, Sarah Sousa
Gloved Against Blood, Cindy Veach
Threshold, Joseph O. Legaspi
Jesus Was a Homeboy, Kevin Carey
Eating Moors and Christians, Sandra M. Castillo
Esther, Pam Bernard
Love's Labors, Brent Newsom
Places I Was Dreaming, Loren Graham
Misery Islands, January Gill O'Neil
Spooky Action at a Distance, Howard Levy
door of thin skins, Shira Dentz
Where the Dead Are, Wanda S. Praisner
Darkening the Grass, Michael Miller
The One Fifteen to Penn Station, Kevin Carey

My Painted Warriors, Peggy Penn
Neighborhood Register, Marcus Jackson
Night Sessions, David S. Cho
Underlife, January Gill O'Neil
The Second Night of the Spirit, Bhisham Bherwani
The Red Canoe: Love In Its Making, Joan Cusack Handler
WE AREN'T WHO WE ARE and this world isn't either, Christine Korfhage
Imago, Joseph O. Legaspi
Through a Gate of Trees, Susan Jackson
Against Which, Ross Gay
The Silence of Men, Richard Jeffrey Newman
The Disheveled Bed, Andrea Carter Brown
The Fork Without Hunger, Laurie Lamon
The Singers I Prefer, Christian Barter
Momentum, Catherine Doty
An Imperfect Lover, Georgianna Orsini
Soft Box, Celia Bland
Rattle, Eloise Bruce
Eyelevel: Fifty Histories, Christopher Matthews
GlOrious, Joan Cusack Handler
The Palace of Ashes, Sherry Fairchok
Silk Elegy, Sondra Gash
So Close, Peggy Penn
Kazimierz Square, Karen Chase
A Day This Lit, Howard Levy

This book was printed on paper from responsible sources.

The text of *The Last Beast We Revel In* was set in Liberation Serif